DRAGON FIELD GUIDES

DRAGON Folklore

A Field Guide

BRIANNA KAISER

Lerner Publications ◆ Minneapolis

For Paul, who grew up loving stories of dragons

Lerner Publications Company
An imprint of Lerner Publishing Group, Inc.
241 First Avenue North
Minneapolis, MN 55401 USA

For reading levels and more information, look up this title at www.lernerbooks.com.

Main body text set in Aptifer Sans LT Pro.
Typeface provided by Linotype AG.

Editor: Annie Zheng **Designer:** Athena Currier **Photo Editor:** Elena Mai
Lerner team: Martha Kranes, Sue Marquis

Library of Congress Cataloging-in-Publication Data

Names: Kaiser, Brianna, 1996– author.
Title: Dragon folklore : a field guide / Brianna Kaiser.
Description: Minneapolis, MN : Lerner Publications, [2026] | Series: Dragon field guides | Includes bibliographical references and index. | Audience: Ages 8–11 | Audience: Grades 4–6 | Summary: "Dragon myths and folklore come from all around the world! Readers discover tales of heroes slaying multi-headed dragons, dragons that formed the universe, and more in this fun, high-interest book"— Provided by publisher.
Identifiers: LCCN 2024043531 (print) | LCCN 2024043532 (ebook) | ISBN 9798765669327 (library binding) | ISBN 9798765683972 (paperback) | ISBN 9798765677018 (epub)
Subjects: LCSH: Dragons—Folklore—Juvenile literature.
Classification: LCC GR830.D7 K33 2026 (print) | LCC GR830.D7 (ebook) | DDC 398.24/54—dc23/eng/20240923

LC record available at https://lccn.loc.gov/2024043531
LC ebook record available at https://lccn.loc.gov/2024043532

Manufactured in the United States of America
1-1011748-53903-1/9/2025

Table of Contents

Powerful Eyes

In the caves of Gambia, the Ninki Nanka hides. The creature has the body of a crocodile, the neck of a giraffe, and three horns. But the most dangerous part of its body is its eyes.

Each Gambian tribe has their own story of the Ninki Nanka. The Mandinka say that anyone who looks in the eyes of the Ninki Nanka gets hypnotized. So the Mandinka carry around a mirror with them. If the Ninki Nanka sees its reflection in the mirror, it dies.

Dragons can be seen as a force of good or evil depending on the folklore they appear in. Sometimes they are neither.

Dragon myths and folklore, such as the folklore of the Mandinka, come from all over the world. For thousands of years, people have told stories of heroes defeating dragons, gods of creation that take the shape of dragons, and dragons using elements of nature.

Dragons can appear in many forms. In some ancient stories, they are large reptiles. What dragon myths or folklore do you know?

CHAPTER 1

Heroes Defeat the Dragons

A common theme of many dragon myths and folklore is heroes coming to the rescue. Whether the dragons have one head or multiple heads, heroes stop them from harming people and villages.

Beating the Hydra

A huge serpent monster with nine heads kept attacking villages. The people fought back. But each time they cut off one of the monster's heads, two more would grow in its place. The monster is known as the Hydra.

A piece of art depicting the battle of Hercules and the Hydra

The Roman hero Hercules, also known as the Greek hero Heracles, decided to help. Hercules was part mortal and part god. He had great strength. Hercules knew the Hydra had one immortal head and that the rest of the heads were mortal.

FACT VS. FICTION

Dragons can have body parts of other animals.

FACT!

Stories of the dragon Tarasque come from Provence, a region in southern France. The dragon had the head of a lion, a turtle shell on its back, six bear paws, and the tail of a serpent. The Tarasque would attack boats and villages by the Rhône River and then hide underwater. Legend has it that Saint Martha defeated the dragon by throwing holy water on it.

A statue of the Tarasque stands in Tarascon, France.

In some stories, Hercules cuts off the Hydra's heads with a sword. In other stories, he uses his hands.

One by one, Hercules kept cutting off the Hydra's mortal heads. Meanwhile, his nephew Iolaus burned the wounds so that no new heads could grow. Finally, only the immortal head was left. Hercules cut it off the monster and buried it.

The Hydra appears in ancient Greek and Roman myths. There are many versions of the story, so the Hydra has not always had the same number of heads.

EIGHT HEADS

In Japanese myth, the dragon Yamata no Orochi has eight heads and tails. The storm god Susanoo beat the dragon.

Yamata no Orochi is a creature that represents chaos and destruction.

Regrowing Heads

A dragon was burning down villages in the northern part of Europe and Asia. A man named Ivan went to the dragon's cave to defeat it. But when Ivan got there, he realized it was no ordinary dragon. It had six heads!

Ivan quickly cut off all the dragon's heads and left. The next night, he returned to the cave to make sure the dragon was dead. But the dragon was still alive, and it now had nine heads. Ivan cut off the heads again.

When Ivan returned the next night, he counted twelve heads! The dragon had used one of its fingers to regrow its heads. Ivan then got his two brothers to help him.

The dragon Ivan fought is an example of a zmei, or zmey, a type of Slavic serpent or dragon. Another zmei is Zmey Gorynych (*above*).

Together, they cut off the dragon's finger before cutting off all the heads. Without the finger, the dragon couldn't grow its heads back.

The dragon in this story is Chudo-Yudo. Chudo-Yudo guards the Slavic underworld.

A KNIGHT'S STORY

The water dragon Knucker of the United Kingdom attacked villages. In one story about Knucker, a knight beat the dragon.

In many tales, knights, demigods, and gods defeat dragons.

An illustration of Ivan cutting off Chudo-Yudo's heads

CHAPTER 2
Power of the Gods

In some myths and folklore, dragons battle gods. In other stories, dragons themselves are powerful gods. Dragons are part of both creation stories and stories about the end of the world.

Stopping the Sun

Ra (also known as Re), the Egyptian god of the sun, sailed through the sky each day. At night, the sun fell from the sky. Ra would then travel through the underworld. There, the demon of chaos would attack Ra.

The demon appeared as a serpentlike dragon. It attacked Ra to try to stop the sun from rising the next day. Ra killed the demon each night so that the sun could rise again. But since the demon was killed in the underworld, it always came back to life and was ready to try to beat Ra the next night.

In ancient Egyptian myth, the demon is known as Apopis, Apophis, or Apep. Apopis is a symbol of evil and the enemy of Ra.

Archaeologists have found hieroglyphics in Egyptian tombs depicting Apopis.

Jörmungandr is often depicted as a large sea monster that lurks in the waters surrounding Midgard.

Battle that Ended the World

The huge serpentine dragon Jörmungandr held its tail in its mouth as it circled Midgard—the Norse human world. But then a battle, known as Ragnarök, erupted. All the forces of chaos fought against the gods.

Jörmungandr joined the forces of chaos and faced Thor, the god of thunder. Thor used his powerful hammer Mjölnir to kill the serpent. But Jörmungandr injected Thor with its poisons before dying, also killing Thor.

In Norse myth, Jörmungandr is also called the Midgard Serpent, or the World Serpent. Ragnarök is a battle that ended the world. Many gods, including Thor, died in the battle. After the world ended, a new world was born.

Thor is considered the protector of humans in Midgard against evil beings.

Creating Chaos

In one Persian myth, Ahura Mazda created all things and ruled over many gods and spirits. But an evil spirit called Angra Mainyu, or Ahriman, liked to spread chaos and confusion. Angra Mainyu created a three-headed dragon to cause chaos.

The dragon had thousands of senses. It could detect any threat and defend itself. But one day, the hero Thraetaona captured the dragon. The dragon was kept in chains until the end of the world.

This dragon is known as Azhi Dahāka. In Persia, dragons are symbols of evil and disorder. Azhi Dahāka is the most powerful Persian dragon.

Ahura Mazda is considered the highest deity in the Zoroastrian religion.

A carving showing Marduk (*right*) battling Tiamat (*left*)

Forming the Universe

Tiamat and Apsu were gods from Mesopotamian myth. Tiamat was the goddess of salt water, and Apsu was the god of fresh water. Together, they created the first gods. More gods followed.

But the family of gods fought, and the fighting turned into war. During the war, the god Marduk killed Tiamat. Marduk separated her body in two. He used one half of her body to form the sun, moon, and stars. The other half of Tiamat's body became the earth.

Tiamat is considered the mother of gods. She has been depicted in many forms in different versions of the story. She has been described as a woman, a body of water, and a dragon.

Lizard Deity of Lahaina

Kihawahine is one of many mo'o in Hawaii's history.

Kihawahine Mokuhinia Kalamaʻula Kalāʻaiheana was born the daughter of Piʻilani and Lāʻieloheloheikawai. Piʻilani was the chief of Maui in the 1500s. Maui is one of the islands of what later became Hawaii.

When Kihawahine died, a chiefess performed a ceremony over her bones. The ceremony turned Kihawahine into a moʻo. Moʻo are lizard deities who protect waterways and ponds. Kihawahine protected the people of Lahaina in Maui.

SHAPESHIFTERS

Stories of Chuvash dragons come from Russia. These dragons can shapeshift into humans and back into dragons.

Mo'o vary in size. They can be as small as a gecko or as big as a mountain. Some stories describe Kihawahine as being a 7-foot (2.1 m) long black dragon with red hair. With her mana, or spiritual power, Kihawahine moved among the islands of Hawaii.

CHAPTER 3

Roaming the Waters and Skies

Dragons around the world live in all kinds of places such as caves, forests, or bodies of water. Some dragons can control elements of nature or are connected to certain elements.

Eating the Moon

The Bakunawa were dragons of the sea in the Philippines. They had two sets of wings, whiskers, and a red tongue. Each night, the dragons would rise out of the sea to eat the seven moons. But when they ate the moons, the sky would darken. People began making noise to stop the Bakunawa from eating the moons, so the sky could stay bright at night.

Some stories say there were multiple dragons, while other stories say it was just one dragon. The stories have been used to describe lunar eclipses. A lunar eclipse happens when Earth travels between the sun and the moon, causing Earth's shadow to fall on the moon's surface.

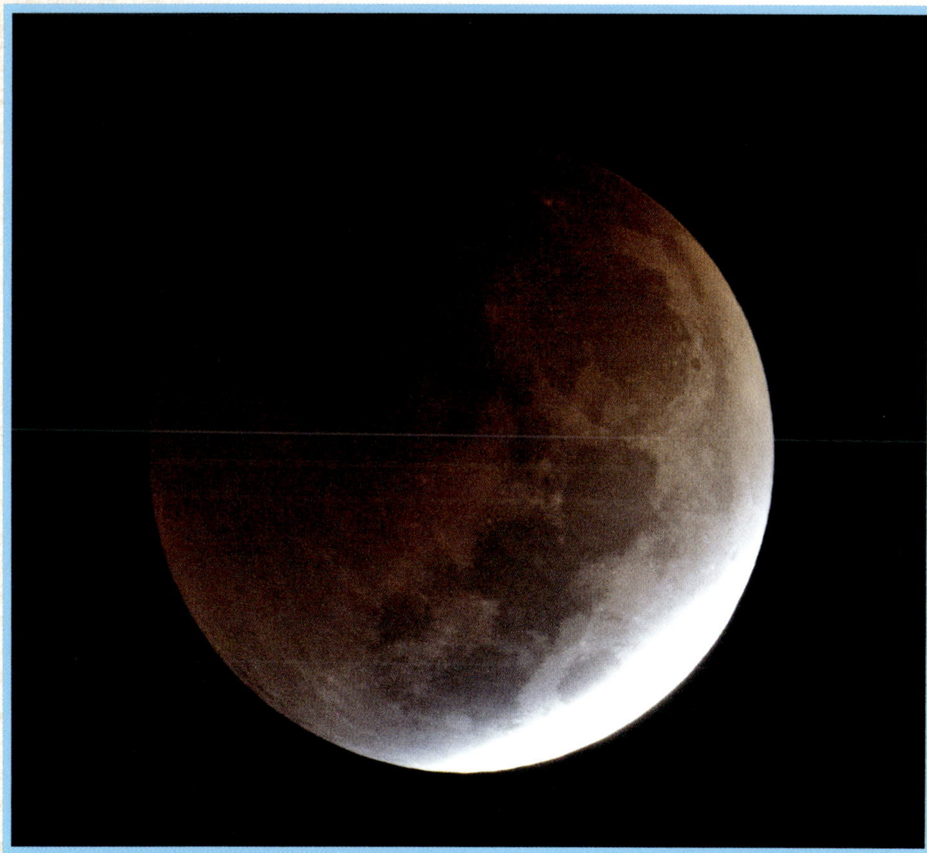

A lunar eclipse from November 2022

Water Dragons

Long, also known as lung or loong, were dragons that lived in bodies of water such as rivers, lakes, and oceans. They had four legs, horns or antlers, claws, and bodies covered in scales. Stories of these dragons come from ancient Chinese myth.

There were four main long. Tianlong was the Celestial Dragon. It guarded the home of the gods. Fuzanglong was the Dragon of Hidden Treasure. Dilong was the Earth Dragon and controlled waterways. Shenlong was the Spiritual Dragon. It controlled wind and rain.

THE METEOR DRAGON

Gaasyendietha, or the meteor dragon, comes from stories of the Seneca. In one story, Gaasyendietha traveled to Earth on a meteor.

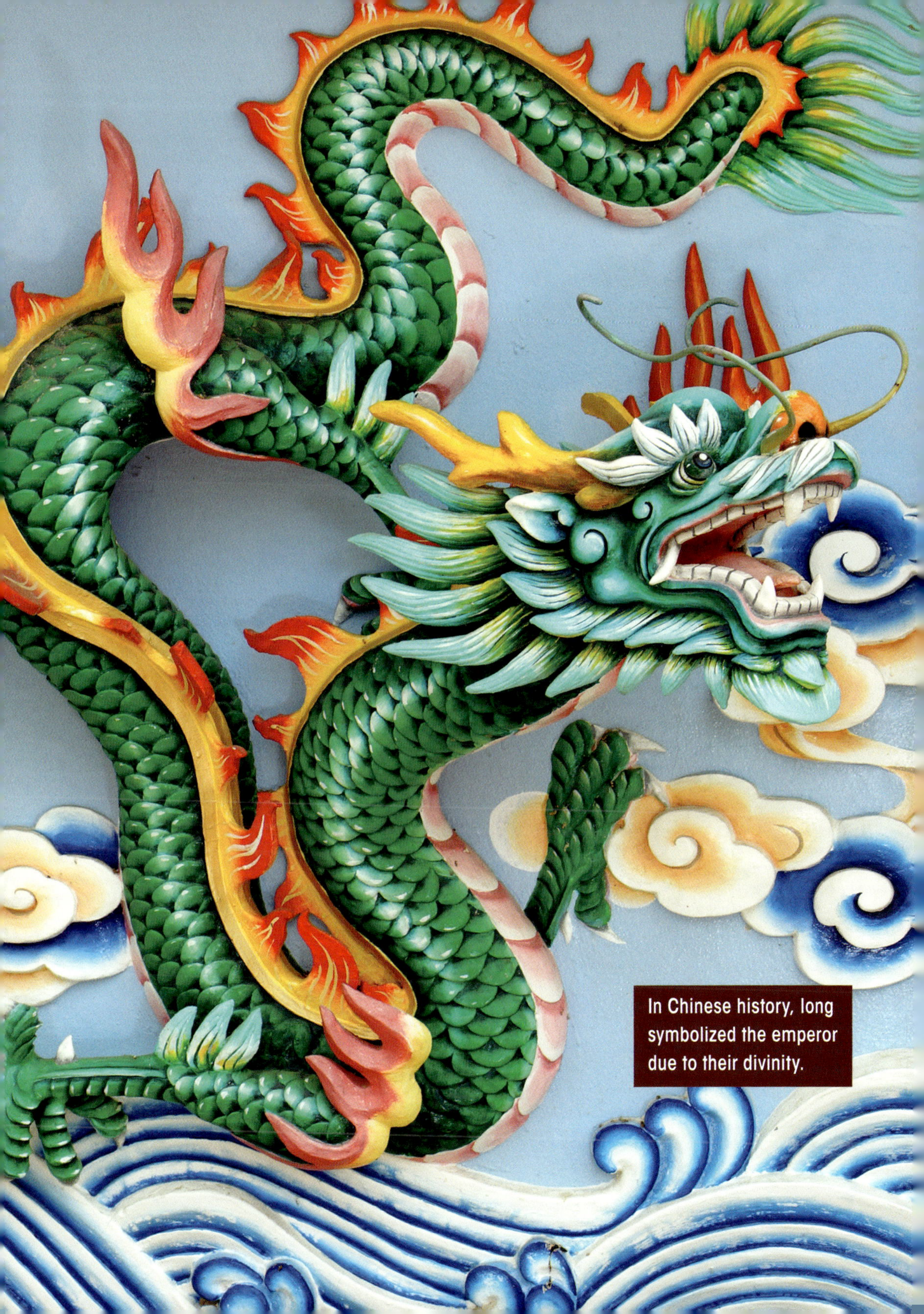

In Chinese history, long symbolized the emperor due to their divinity.

Rainbow Serpents

In Australia, a huge serpentine dragon traveled from one river or waterhole to the next. When it traveled, a rainbow appeared. Rainbow Serpents appear in stories of many Aboriginal tribes. The stories vary, but the serpents are often powerful and connected to water.

An Aboriginal rock painting of a Rainbow Serpent found in Australia

One of the Rainbow Serpents was Kanmare, a huge water serpent with a head of hair. The Mitakoodi called this serpent Tulloun. The Kabi tell stories about Dhakkan. Dhakkan was a powerful creature that was a hybrid of a fish and snake. The Bakanji tell stories of Neitee and Yeutta—big snake creatures with large teeth.

Your Turn

Now that you've heard some dragon folklore from around the world, what do you think? Did you have a favorite story? Do you know any dragon folklore that was not included in this book?

Talk about your favorite dragon stories with a friend. People have been telling stories of dragons for thousands of years. Compare your stories. Maybe your stories have similar themes such as a hero defeating the dragon. Or maybe your favorite story is unlike any other.

A Look at Quetzalcóatl

In one Mesoamerican creation story, the god Quetzalcóatl worked with Tezcatlipoca to create the world. They turned themselves into huge snakes resembling dragons and ripped apart the serpent Tlaltecuhtli, or Cipactli. They then used one part of the monster's body to create the earth and the other part to create the sky. Quetzalcóatl is known as the Feathered Serpent and appears in Aztec and Mayan folklore.

A statue of Quetzalcóatl

Glossary

ancient: very old, or relating to a time early in history

deity: a god

element: a force of nature, such as air or water

folklore: the beliefs, customs, and stories of a community that are passed down through generations

hypnotize: to capture a person's complete attention

immortal: a person or creature that lives forever

myth: a story often with imaginative creatures, people, and events that explain history, beliefs, or something else

symbol: an object that represents something else

underworld: a place where people or spirits in some cultures may go after they die

Learn More

Bell, Samantha. *Dragons of Chinese Mythology*. Minneapolis: Kids Core, 2023.

Britannica Kids: Apopis
https://kids.britannica.com/students/article/Apopis/309768

Britannica Kids: Hydra
https://kids.britannica.com/students/article/Hydra/624607

Fenmore, Taylor. *Dragons around the World: A Field Guide*. Minneapolis: Lerner Publications, 2026.

Kiddle: Bakunawa Facts for Kids
https://kids.kiddle.co/Bakunawa

Rea, Amy C. *Dragons of Norse Mythology*. Minneapolis: Kids Core, 2024.

Index

Photo Acknowledgments

Image credits: MassanPH/Getty Images, p. 5; Heritage Image Partnership Ltd/Alamy, p. 7; Hal Beral/Getty Images, p. 8; KUCO/Shutterstock, p. 9; Yukari MISHIMA/Shutterstock, p. 10; Chronicle/Alamy, p. 11; peepo/Getty Images, p. 12; Album/Alamy, p. 13; Rafa Barcelos/Shutterstock, p. 15; Hatteviden/Shutterstock, p. 16; fotokostic/Getty Images, p. 17; suronin/Shutterstock, p. 18; Ivy Close Images/Alamy, p. 19; Wolfgang Sauber/Wikimedia Commons (Creative Commons Attribution-Share Alike 4.0), p. 20; NASA/Joel Kowsky, p. 23; dangdumrong/Getty Images, p. 25; mauritius images GmbH/Alamy, p. 26; Smith Archive/Alamy, p. 29. Design elements: NikonLamp/Shutterstock; Lukasz Szwaj/Shutterstock; vi73/Shutterstock; T Studio/Shutterstock; VartB/Shutterstock.

Cover: Barashkova Natalia/Shutterstock.